Jealous

A CHERRYTREE BOOK

This edition first published in 2007
by Cherrytree Books, part of
The Evans Publishing Group Limited
2A Portman Mansions
Chiltern St
London
W1U 6NR

© Evans Brothers Ltd 2007

Printed in Malaysia

British Library Cataloguing in Publication Data
Amos, Janine
    Jealous. - 2nd ed. - (Feelings)
    1. Jealousy - Juvenile literature 2. Envy - Juvenile literature
    I. Title
    155.4'1248

ISBN 978 184234453 8
First published in paperback1997

CREDITS
Editor: Louise John
Designer: D. R. ink
Production: Jenny Mulvanny

VISIT OUR WEBSITE
Evans
www.evansbooks.co.uk

Jealous

By Janine Amos
Illustrated by Gwen Green

CHERRYTREE BOOKS

Kelly's story

"Hurry up!" called Kelly's dad. "You'll be late!"

Kelly's dad always took Kelly and her sister to school. But today Kelly was on her own. Sarah had chickenpox.

"What will Sarah do all day?" asked Kelly.

"She'll stay in bed and sleep a lot," said Kelly's dad.

Kelly climbed into the car.

"Will Mum stay with her?" she asked.

"Yes," said Kelly's dad, "Mum will look after her."

"I expect Mum will read her stories," said Kelly. "I expect they'll eat toast and drink hot chocolate together." Kelly's dad smiled. But Kelly didn't think it was funny.

When Kelly came in from school she ran up to Sarah's bedroom. Sarah was asleep. She looked very warm and cosy. On the bed there were two big storybooks and a new comic.

"I wish I had chickenpox," thought Kelly.

Why did Kelly wish she had chickenpox?

After tea, Aunty Mary came to visit. She had brought Sarah a
Get Well card and some grapes. Kelly liked grapes.
"I don't feel well, either!" said Kelly. But everyone laughed.

Kelly took the grapes upstairs. Sarah was still asleep. Her face was red and spotty. Kelly sat at the end of Sarah's bed. She looked at the grapes – they were fat, green ones, with no pips. Slowly Kelly popped a grape into her mouth. Then she had another. Soon there were only two grapes left.

Was Kelly hungry?
Why do you think she ate the grapes?

Kelly went into her own room. She felt cross. She was cross with herself for eating the grapes, and she was cross with Sarah for being ill.

Just then, Kelly's dad came in. He sat down next to Kelly. But he didn't smile.

"You're not very kind to your little sister, are you?" said Kelly's dad. "Last week you spoilt her drawing. Yesterday you broke her doll, and today you've eaten her grapes." Kelly went red.

"Why do you do it, Kelly?" asked her dad.

Why do you think Kelly was unkind to Sarah
How does Kelly feel now

9

Kelly's dad waited. It was very quiet. Kelly could hear the clock ticking. She knew it was important to talk.

"Sarah always gets everything," Kelly said at last. "You and Mum are always talking about her. You don't care about me!"

Kelly's dad put his arm around her.

"I'm sorry you feel like that," he said. "But you're wrong. Mum and I love you both. We have to do more things for Sarah – she's only five. But we love you just as much." Kelly's dad smiled. "Wait here!" he said.

Kelly's dad came back with a big box. Inside there were lots of photographs. Kelly's dad pointed to one of them.

"That's you," he said to Kelly, "with chickenpox. You were two years old."

"I thought people only took photographs at birthdays or on holiday," said Kelly.

"Not always," said her dad.

Together they looked at the picture.

"I had lots of spots," said Kelly, laughing.

Why do you think Kelly's dad showed her the photographs?

Kelly looked at all the photographs in the box. Some were of her mum. Some were of Aunty Mary and Gran. But most of them were of Kelly when she was a very little girl.

"Did you take all these photographs of me?" asked Kelly.

"Yes," said her dad. "Tomorrow we'll buy a photograph album and fix them in."

"Great!" said Kelly.

Before bedtime, Kelly gave her dad a big hug.
"Can we take some photographs tomorrow?" she asked.
"Yes," said Kelly's dad. "Who shall we photograph?"
"Sarah, of course – with chickenpox!" said Kelly.

How do you think Kelly feels now?

Feeling like Kelly

Have you ever felt like Kelly?
It's called feeling jealous.
Jealousy is a powerful feeling.
It may make you sad, cross
and lonely too. It never makes
you happy.

Jealousy grows

Jealousy can grow. It grows in
your imagination. Kelly was
jealous of Sarah. She
imagined Sarah having a good
time – even when she was ill.

Jealousy spoils things

Jealousy can spoil things. It can spoil friendships. If you think someone has something you haven't, you may want to hurt them. Kelly thought her parents loved Sarah best. That's why she was unkind to her sister. But being unkind didn't help Kelly. It only made her feel cross with herself.

Think about it

Read the stories in this book. Think about the people in them. Do you feel like them sometimes? Next time you feel jealous, ask yourself some questions. What am I jealous of? Am I really missing out? Who can I talk to, to make me feel better?

Danny's story

It was Christmas morning! Danny opened his eyes and jumped out of bed.

"Wake up, Luke!" he shouted to his cousin. "I'll race you downstairs."

Luke was two years older than Danny. But he was just as excited about Christmas. The two boys pulled on their jeans and ran across the landing.

"Less noise, you two!" called a grown-up.

But Danny and Luke didn't hear. They were already halfway down the stairs, heading for the big Christmas tree. All their presents would be underneath it – waiting to be opened.

Soon the floor was covered in wrapping paper – and toys. Then Luke jumped up. He ran across to the other end of the room. There, side by side, were two huge parcels.

"Quick, Danny!" he shouted. "There's one each."

It was hard work to open the parcel. But soon Danny had done it, and in front of him stood a brand new bike. Tied onto the handlebars was a message:

Happy Christmas Danny, from Mum and Dad.

"Just what I wanted!" said Danny.

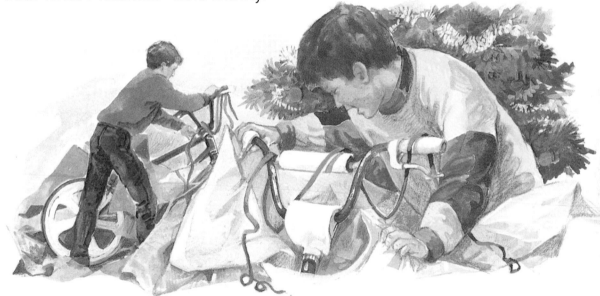

How do you think Danny feels

Danny turned to watch Luke. Luke was just pulling his bike out of its wrappings. Danny opened his eyes wide. It was the most beautiful bike he'd ever seen! It was blue with white wheels and a red seat. And on the side was painted "Road Tiger".

"I wish I had that bike," thought Danny.

Soon everyone else was awake. They all came down to see the boys' presents.

"Aren't you two boys lucky?" said Luke's dad.

"I'm going straight out after breakfast," said Luke. "I can't wait to ride the Road Tiger."

"I'll come out later," said Danny.

How is Danny feeling now?
Have you ever felt like this?

Danny watched Luke wheel the Road Tiger out of the door. Then he looked at his pile of presents and his new red bike. Danny had everything he'd asked for. He knew he should be happy. But instead he felt cross.

"Why does Luke get everything?" he thought. "It's not fair."

All day Danny stayed inside. He did a jigsaw puzzle and he watched television. He played a game with his uncle, and he thought about the blue and white Road Tiger. The more he thought about the bike, the more he wanted to ride it.

Just before bedtime, Danny crept into the dark hallway. He put his hand on the Road Tiger's shiny frame.

"Danny!" said a voice.

Danny jumped. It was his mum.

"I was only looking," said Danny quickly. "I wasn't doing anything wrong. Honestly."

What do you think Danny's mum will say?

"So you wish you had Luke's bike, do you?" asked Danny's mum. Danny didn't know what to say.

"Don't worry," said Danny's mum. "Everyone feels like that sometimes – grown-ups too. It's natural."

"It's not a nice feeling," said Danny.

"I know," said his mum. "But try to enjoy what you have. Go for a ride with Luke tomorrow. Your bike may not be a Road Tiger, but it works just as well."

It was true. Danny looked at his red bike and smiled.

"It's got a name, too," said Danny.

"What's that?" asked his mum.

"I'll call it the Street Fox!" said Danny.

Feeling like Danny

Have you ever wanted something that belonged to someone else? Have you ever thought that something your sister, brother or friend had was nicer than anything you owned? I expect you have – most people do sometimes, adults too. It's often hard to know what to do about it. You start to think, "It's not fair!"

What can you do?

When you're feeling like this, it helps to think of all the ways in which you are lucky. You could make a list of all the things that make you feel good. Or you could try talking about your feelings with someone you trust – just as Danny did.

Kate's story

Kate and Jenny were walking home from school. Their bags were heavy and it was very hot. But Kate and Jenny didn't notice. They were planning what to do after tea.

"You could come to my house," said Jenny.

"Let's go to the park," said Kate.

"And what shall we play?" Jenny asked.

"Witches!" they both shouted together.

Kate and Jenny were best friends. Their parents were friends too. Kate and Jenny went to the same school. They liked the same things, and their favourite game was Witches.

After tea, Kate called for Jenny.

"Let's go!" said Kate. She was excited.

"Wait a minute," said Jenny.

"Why are we waiting?" asked Kate.

"Kim's coming," said Jenny. "I asked her."

Kate was cross.

"We don't need her," she said.

"I like her," said Jenny.

"Well, I don't," said Kate. "We can't play Witches now."

"Yes we can," Jenny said. "We'll have three witches."

Why is Kate cross?

Soon Kim arrived. She was puffing.

"Sorry I'm late!" said Kim.

Jenny smiled. She put her arm through Kim's. But Kate didn't smile. She stuck her hands in her pockets and turned away.

On the way to the park, Kate was very quiet. She walked behind Jenny and Kim and watched them.

"Jenny likes Kim more than me," she thought. She kicked a stone with her foot.

How does Kate feel?
If you were Kate, what would you do now?

Jenny told Kim all about the game.

"You can be Chief Witch," she said. "You've got the longest hair." Kate looked at Kim's hair. It was long and curly. Kate wished she could give Kim a hard smack.

"I hate Kim," she thought.

The next day, Kate felt sad. When she got to school, Jenny was in the playground. Kim was there too and they were laughing. Kate didn't go up to them. She didn't even say hello.

Why doesn't Kate talk to Jenny and Kim?

At playtime, Kate felt worse. She wanted to cry. Kate's teacher, Mr Rose, asked her what was wrong.

"Kim's taken my friend away," said Kate sadly. And she told him about Jenny and Kim. "I'm on my own."

"You don't have to be," said Mr Rose. "You can join in with Jenny and Kim. We have to share our friends, Kate – just as we share other things."

Kate thought for a while.

"Shall we go across and say hello?" asked Mr Rose.

So Kate and Mr Rose walked over to where Jenny and Kim were playing.

When Kate and Mr Rose arrived, Jenny and Kim smiled.

"Can I play with you?" asked Kate, quietly.

"Of course!" said Kim. She put her arm through Kate's, and Jenny took Kate's other arm.

"What are you going to play?" asked Mr Rose.

"WITCHES!" shouted Kate, Jenny and Kim together.

How did Mr Rose help Kate?

Feeling like Kate

Have you ever felt like Kate? Sometimes it's hard to share your friends. You want to keep them to yourself. But people aren't like toys – you can't own them.

Making friends

When Jenny asked Kim to play, Kate felt cross. She was a bit scared too. She was scared that Jenny didn't like her any more. If someone makes a new friend, it doesn't mean they like you less. It's just that they like someone else as well!

Talking about it

Jealousy can make you sad and lonely. If you're feeling like this, tell someone. Talk to someone you trust. Kate's teacher knew just how she felt. Someone will understand how you feel too.

Feeling jealous

Think about the stories in this book. Kelly, Danny and Kate all felt jealous. Talking about it helped them. It could help you.

If you are feeling frightened or unhappy, don't keep it to yourself. Talk to an adult you can trust, like a parent or a teacher. If you feel really alone, you could telephone one of these offices. Remember, there is always someone who can help.

ChildLine
Freephone 0800 1111

The Line
ChildLine helpline for young people living away from home
Freephone 0800 884444
3.30pm to 9.30pm (weekdays)
2pm to 8pm (weekends)

NSPCC Child Protection Line
Phone 0808 800 5000

The Samaritans
Phone 08457 909090